TWO PIANOS, FOUR HANDS – INTERMEDIATE LEVEL

COMPOSER
SHOWCASE
HAL LEONARD
STUDENT PIANO LIBRARY

Jambalaya

A Portrait of Old New Orleans

FOR TWO PIANOS, FOUR HANDS

BY EUGÉNIE ROCHEROLLE

ISBN 978-1-4234-3809-0

HAL•LEONARD®
CORPORATION

7777 W. BLUEMOUND RD. P.O. BOX 13819 MILWAUKEE, WI 53213

In Australia Contact:
Hal Leonard Australia Pty. Ltd.
4 Lentara Court
Cheltenham, Victoria, 3192 Australia
Email: ausadmin@halleonard.com.au

Visit Hal Leonard Online at
www.halleonard.com

Jambalaya

A Portrait of Old New Orleans

Remembering New Orleans the way she used to be,
and the victims of the storm who have had to say goodbye.

By Eugénie Rocherolle

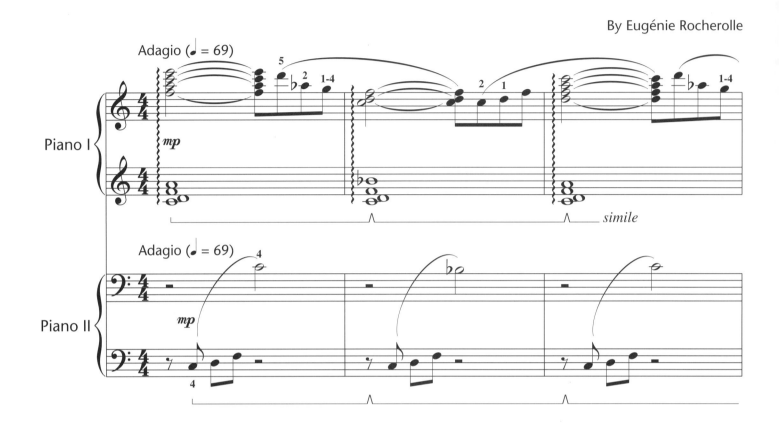

TWO PIANOS, FOUR HANDS – INTERMEDIATE LEVEL

Jambalaya
A Portrait of Old New Orleans

FOR TWO PIANOS, FOUR HANDS

BY EUGÉNIE ROCHEROLLE

HAL•LEONARD®
CORPORATION

7777 W. BLUEMOUND RD. P.O. BOX 13819 MILWAUKEE, WI 53213

Jambalaya

A Portrait of Old New Orleans

Remembering New Orleans the way she used to be,
and the victims of the storm who have had to say goodbye.

By Eugénie Rocherolle

3

15

19

16